A Little Bit O' This And A Little Bit O' That

A collection of poems by

AngieD

GW00458636

Thanks to God, and to all those willing victims of verse over the years who turned that frown into a smile as a result!

WHAT'S IN HERE?

FOREWORD

We live in an imperfect world, none of us are flawless, things go awry every day and, no matter how thorough or careful we are, accidents or mishaps will occur.

Some things are changeable; others are tolerated. The following verses share some of the thoughts and experiences on the journey through the life of the writer thus far.

It is hoped at least one verse will raise a smile from the reader!

(Oh, and by the way, if you notice a change of font – it's deliberate. Just signposting a switch to a slightly different type of poem)

STUFF HAPPENS – SUCH IS LIFE!

THE SQUATTER!

Feels like a fly's <u>up</u> my nose
It's being a tease
Tickling me rotten
And making me sneeze

I'm blowing for England
To try and get free
This foreign body
That's annoyng me

So, as I spray and steam
I pray that I out
This unwanted irritation
From within my snout!

FOOTLOOSE

Where's the foot
That fits the shoe
The one that once walked
Down that avenue

Doesn't the owner realise
It's not there
That one foot is covered
And the other one is bare

It's starting to rain
And all in my mind
Is how can someone not notice
They've left their shoe behind!

FORGET, FORGET NOT

Society has me paranoid
That I'm ignoring the sign
Am I just tired, stupid
Or losing my mind!?

I can't fathom if my forgetfulness
Is no longer that
Whether it's lack of concentration
Or m'brain's become detached

There're lots of things
I forget to do
Is it just me
Or does it happen to you?

Sometimes I try going through the glass door
Not realising it's closed
Bashing my face
And nearly breaking my nose

Other times I eat a yoghurt
And not stop to think
Then put the spoon in the bin
And the empty carton in the sink

When I make and then bake
My apple crumble or pie
I realise it's not in the oven
But in the cupboard close by

Am I the only one ever
To have gone to find
An item in another room
Then it's gone clear out of my mind

I've sprayed hair lacquer under arm
Used soap for lotion
Which when rubbed in has caused
Quite a frothy bubbly commotion!

The night mask I mistook
For rejuvenating cream
Was serum for shiny hair
At least my face had a healthy sheen!

If I forget 'cause of stress
Or I'm in a hurry
Is the fact I sometimes can't remember names
Due cause for worry?

I know not

But please promise if you witness me
Trying to stuff my nose
With spare ribs, spinach
And roast potatoes

Please, please I beg you
Waste no time
In using y'mobile
And ringing 9 9 9!

OFF SIDE

My right foot's gained weight
'Cause my shoe doesn't fit
It travels the same way as the left
Yet it holds a foot and a bit

It gets the same exercise as the left
Also the same meals
The toes collectively get one third
The instep a third, and also both heels

But the question is forever
Embedded on my brain
Why the left foot and the right one
Aren't exactly the same

But if I'm not lopsided
And no one sees
Who cares if one side is larger
Than the other side of me?

NUTS TO YOU!

Will someone PLEASE take
These peanuts away quick
Or I shall finish the packet
And then be sick

They're rather moreish
And I can't leave'em alone
It's not a large packet
And I could down the lot on my own

But that would be piggish
And not ladylike to eat
So many nuts
No matter how sweet

There's half a packet left
Please take'em away
Before I submit to temptation
And scoff the lot today!

LOSE THE WEED, KEEP THE HAIR!

Weeds have such an ability
Like nothing else I know
For without help or nourishment
They never fail to grow

We may have wind or rain
Intense heat or cold
They survive – don't get burned
And their leaves don't seem t'get mould

They've strength greater than tarmac
Concrete or brick
Can rise up above the earth no matter
How dense or thick

Whether torrential downpour
Or intense fire
They won't drown, won't scorch
But rise up from the mire

And then there's hair
Equally as strong
It flies and can adhere to
Where it doesn't belong

It'll stick to your clothes
Like butter to bread
But try keeping it where it should be
On top of y'head!

RUBBISH, RUBBISH!

Why do I have to pick up?
Most other people's trash
I wouldn't mind if it was waste
That I could turn into cash

The sort that's someone's rubbish
But now it's my treasure
That would make me more than smile
Make me a lady of leisure

But I'm just cleaning debris
That's obviously not mine
Beer cans and cigarette ends
Empty bottles of wine

Now, can you see my blood boil
Hear my irritation
Clean your own darn mess before you see
A mad dog impersonation!

MY POSTBOX

Who moved the post-box?
It never was that far
I'm not even half way, my knee's hurting
Now I wish I'd driven the car

I'm trying to adjust my face
So passers-by won't know
How this blinking walk's causing more aggravation
Than I am willing to show

It's bad enough that the mask
Makes it hard for me to breathe
Which, puzzlingly affects my walking
And my ability to see

Then, the glasses perched on my nose
To keep out the sunshine glare
Get misty and all fogged up
'Cause of contained exhaled air

How much further is this post-box?
I'm sure it never was this far
Stuff what anyone says to walk to keep fit
My brain is healthier driving the car!

GET IT STRAIGHT

I never know how
When watching tv
I can slide all the way down
My three-seater settee

I'm propped up straight
I've made sure of that
Have the assistance of cushions
Right where I'm sat

Can't feel myself moving
I don't even flinch
I don't even feel my muscles move
Not even one inch

Yet after a few minutes
I'm almost on the floor
My head's not supported by cushions
Any more

I think I need a seat belt
Or a suitable surround
To safely strap me in
So I don't slip to the ground!

WINTER'S HERE!

It's so cold
It feels like it should be snowing
But the hedges are still green
They haven't stopped growing

It's freezing cold
Y'limbs won't shift
And getting anything to move
Is now both a talent and a gift

One, as my mother would say
Takes it gingerly – to rise from the chair
Which you could've sworn – was much higher
When you first sat there

Now it's a "1-2-3" heave y'self up
'til legs are straight
But to get the back in upright position
Will be a few minutes wait!

Making each step
With sufficient pause
Just in case one walks too quickly
And abruptly falls

I wish we could grow up just a little bit
And not all the way
So limbs didn't creak
And groan all day

So we could continually enjoy
What we've struggled hard to obtain
Without the burden of medication to numb
Each growing pain!

DRESSING DOWN

I thought it felt funny
But I didn't know what was wrong
After all, it was nothing unusual
I've done it all along

I did it in the dark
But that wasn't a factor
I normally did it without looking
That didn't matter

But it was when switching on the light
To prevent a fall
That I checked and saw
It wasn't right at all

I looked at what I was wearing
And quickly found
I'd put my jumper on
Upside down!

MY TIME TO WASTE!

It's easy to sit and do nothing
And enjoy the fact
That no one can tell me to get back to work
No one can say I am sacked!

There's nowt wrong in doing nothing
It's not illegal, it's not a crime
But why do others make me feel guilty
Just 'cause I seem to be wasting MY time!

SWEET HOLIDAY!

To stay at home
When everyone else is away
Is my perfect idea
Of a holiday

I don't have to drive
And get stuck in queues
I don't have to pack
Taking far too many shoes

I can open my window
My back door too
And hear nothing but birds
Chirping through

Sit in my lounge chair
With the drink of my choice
Not queuing at a bar shouting
At the top of my voice

Nope! They can all go on holiday
What I want's right here
My music, peace and quiet
And a cool glass of beer!

WONDERBRA!

It's three days now
Since I lost my bra
It's a sports one, my favourite
Above all the others by far

This recent loss
Is hard to comprehend
Is taking up time
And irritating me no end

It doesn't have wires
To poke and prod
Thus causing discomfort
To this God-given bod

I've searched cupboards, wardrobe
Washing machine
Retraced each step
Into every room I've been

This misplacement of attire's
Making me see red
I know it's not there
But I've even looked under the bed

I'm wondering when washed
It got stuck in trouser leg or cardi sleeve
And trailed behind me
When I went to leave

So I shall check outside
And down the street
And, if seen, shall pick up
Real discreet!

GET THEE BEHIND ME CRITTERS!

I hate between spring
And summer time
When it begins to get warmer
And you see the signs

When the weeds start to grow
And insects wake
And invade your home
As if they own the place

They run round as though
They part own
Your mortgaged-to-the-hilt
Expensive home

They take full advantage
Of the expanse of the place
Entering most rooms
Infiltrating every space

Like every new home
We all like to embark
On putting our own stamp
And they certainly leave their mark

They're fantastic weavers
And second to none
But it's my home so leave
And take the web that you've spun!

HOME IS WHERE THE HEAT IS

I snuggle up in bed
'til the heating clicks on
And don't dare surface 'til
That morning chill has gone

I don't care what day
Or hour it is
Lying here waiting for warmth
Is absolute bliss

I lay and watch tv
Play scrabble on my phone
Don't need to take a plane
I can be warm at home

I may have a huge bill
But not even that can compete
To the beautiful cuddly feeling
Of a home with heat!

HOT MUSIC!

The piano nearly burned down my house
Well a pie was partly at fault
It was warming up in the microwave

And just fine for a few minutes, or so I thought

So I popped to the other room
To practice a song
I didn't think I was there
For very long

But it was quite evident
Pretty soon
That something was not right
In another room

I quickly left my practicing
Back to the kitchen to check
BLOW ME DOWN, it was full of smoke
And quickly began to collect

And gather in the hallway
Filtering through
Into the lounge
And up the stairs too

I took immediate action
Since it was making me cough
And I didn't want to set
The smoke detector off!

The pie was well shot
So too the plastic plate
It wasn't me it was the pie or piano
That was the fault of this fate!

LEG IN LEG OUT!

I wore the wrong leggings
They just won't stay put
I keep pulling 'em up
B'they just end up at my foot

They're brand spanking new
So the elastic shouldn't be shot
So they ought to stay up
I don't know why they're not

I'm way too far from home
So I just can't go and change
So I'll have to continue pulling up while I walk
And tolerate folk looking at me strange!

MACHINE V WOMAN

How can a dishwasher wash dishes
Better than me
Does it have eyes in there
So it can see

Does it check each plate
Fork, spoon, cup
To ensure it's sufficiently clean
And thoroughly washed up?

How can a washing machine wash clothes
Cleaner than me
Can the rotation of the drum wash
More efficiently

I can see what I'm doing
And the bits that need a good rub
How can a machine with no eyes see parts
In need of a thorough scrub

Though I'll continue with man's invention
I'm not completely resigned
That a machine can wash any better
Than these two hands of mine!

BITS 'N' PIECES

Crumbs n dust, crumbs n dust
I'd like to live in a world without
Crumbs n dust

You can sweep 'n' polish to your heart's delight
But don't think you're ever gonna
Win the fight

Dust 'n' crumbs, dust 'n' crumbs
What a blessing to live without
Dust 'n' crumbs

My life would be blissful if I could only just
Find a world that existed
Without crumbs n dust!

FEAR – AN EXPENSIVE PAST TIME!

I was playing on my keyboard
Whilst scanning the walls
To ensure all that was black was inanimate
And did not crawl

When something moved
In the space quite near
Which made me jump
And knock the keyboard clear

Broom to hand
I bashed the wall
Missing that thing
But that wasn't all

A picture came down
Glass and frame
And what I uttered next
Filled me full of shame

The tambourine followed
But what made me sore
Was the splinters of glass
All over the floor

More expletives followed
I have to confess
'Cause it took what seemed hours
To clear up the mess!

DRIVER'S PREROGATIVE?

Our roads present daily challenges; other drivers, speed bumps etc all give us reason at some time to count to ten!

LEARNER'S ISLAND

Please show me the driving instructor
Who regularly taught
Their students to park
Without due care and thought

The one who instructs
Their pupil to ignore
And just drive over a roundabout
Never mind the law

Show me the instructor
Who prepares for a test
Stating that never giving a signal to turn
Is always best

Or the instructor who thinks
It's perfectly okay
For students to drive 15mph
Obstructing my way

Please forgive if I secretly wish
That some Divine Hand
Would whisk these instructors and their students off
To a remote faraway land!

UMPER BUMPER

As I sit in the middle back seat
On this lump
Experiencing every single part
Of every single bump

It's no easy ride
For my now sore rump
Which is now converting me
Into a right moany grump

I do wish someone
Would come up trumps
For another way to stop folk speeding
Than those uncomfortable humps!

AND THE BEAT GOES ON!

Our country is nothing but
Cameras and bumps
They happily watch
As you manoeuvre each hump

There're very few roads I drive
Where my CDs don't jump
That when your rear leaves the seat
It returns with a thump

The bop you do
Is not necessarily in time
But you'll have plenty of opportunities
To keep on trying

'Cause I'm sure they're not done
With humping each street
Perhaps they're waiting for us all
To bump to the beat!

AND ANOTHER ONE!

O-ohh – a slow driver at the front
And we all form a queue
Waiting patiently to drive on
Is all I can do

Turn up my music
As loud as I can
To block all impatience
From reaching my hand

Moving it from steering
And so highlight my scorn
When it impulsively and continually
Honks the horn!

I hope they who are driving
Is suitably impressed
That I'm still in my car
Though not free from stress

And, as I wait in line
I can't help but feel
My life's getting shorter
As I sit motionless behind this wheel!

NO WAY FOR LEARNERS!

Do you know how many learners
I saw today – 9!
It should be law that there should be no more
Than one on the road at a time

'Cause, add to that a bus, taxi,
And a ten wheeled truck
And I'm in traffic limbo
Like a pig in muck!

I've just enough patience to travel
From A to B
For a couple of minutes
Or maybe three

But four learner drivers
Bumper to boot
Is definitely not
My preferred route

I need to download the App
That sounds an alarm
When learners are on the road
So I can change direction and keep calm!

BOPPITY BOP!

If we were meant to bop
Up and down
Then why give us feet
To walk on ground

If our rears were built
To be continually beat
Then they would have been cushioned
For contact with the seat

For the purposes of car travel
We should have been
Fitted with a couple of
Mobile trampolines

So this sensitive part
Of my anatomy
Would be protected from the impact
Of road humps on me

Hmmm... on the other hand...

Perhaps a higher being is privy
To what's in my mind
And knows the vehicular vibrations
Will do wonders for my behind!

STRESSES AND STRAINS: TRAVELLING BY BUS TUBE OR TRAIN

Daily commuting has brought its own share of amusing sights and thoughts, from waking up to the end destination; whether walking to the station, on the platform, in the train or looking through the window, all present a reason to write......

NO NOISE PLEASE!

The train was so blissful
Travelling yesterday
Everyone sat quietly
Or read away

No telephones no friends
Wanting to chat
How I wish each morning's journey
Was as quiet as that

But now someone's playing music
And it's beginning to bug
Someone should be brave
And pull his plug!

STUCK ON YOU!

It's hard to find a seat
That doesn't come equipped
With gum, chocolate, mud
Or dried up day old sick

And it's hard to find a seat
That's not loose when you sit down
And that when the train is moving
It doesn't fling you to the ground!

BACK TO SQUARE ONE!

My normal train was cancelled
Then the one after that
Was ram jam packed
With no space to swing a cat

So, in order to get a seat
You had to push your way on
'Cause if you didn't you'd've ended up
Right back where you started from!

NICE SUN, BUT NOT NOW!

I'm not ungrateful
I do like the sun
But not when I'm late
And I have to run

It takes no prisoners
And sometimes I think
Either I stay cool and miss the train
Or I catch it, and stink!

THE NEW DAY

I came out this morning
And there was not a soul in sight
But one cyclist, one shop owner
And the stars of the night

The car was wet
With the freshness of dew
And the darkness began to fade
So the light was showing through

I looked up to the sky
Now with patches of white
Where last night was giving way
To the morning light

Another day to travel
On that nasty old train
And ten hours in the office
Before I'm back home again!

ANOTHER DELAY!

There's nothing I can do
But oh the frustration
The train's stopped again
Between another station

I won't say anything
I won't make a fuss
But if I wanted to take this long
I'D HAVE TAKEN THE BUS!

NICE – JUST NICE!

The mist sits firmly
Topping the fields
With cows searching hungrily
For their morning meals

The view, though the same
Just a little more blue than grey
Is far more breathtaking
Than it was yesterday!

UNSTIRRABLE!

Some days I wake up
Full of zest
And think this day
Will be one of my best

And other days I think
Why bother to get up
From a slumber which would be criminal
To let anything interrupt!

GREAT JOURNEY!

Not a murmur not a stir
No loud conversation
No MP3s or mobiles
To cause irritation

No sneezing, clearing throats
Not even a cough
I'm almost thinking this morning
That I don't want to get off!

GET DOWN BOOGIE!

He had a drip
On the end of his nose
And he stuck out his tongue
To intercept the flow

After a while I casually
Turned to look
To the man on my left
Reading his book

But that protrusion from his nose
I'd rather not have seen
Big and crusty
Yucky and green

I'm just worried if he sneezes
Or the train suddenly stops
That the boogie he's wearing
Might sideways drop!

MISSED IT!

I had to run
For the bus today
And as I prepared to get on
It didn't stop – but just drove away

The bus stop was full
Before I came
So I daren't look back
Because of my shame!

ONE MAN SHOW!

I thought I'd picked my feet up
But the timing must've been out
And I'm glad when I made my trip
Not many people were about

'Cause normally at the station
There's a never-ending queue
Going in one end and out the other
And doubling up into two

But I'm glad they all were late
And missed my morning show
And, if you don't whisper in their shell like
Then they'll never ever know!

TRESPLENDOUS!

How majestic the trees
I can scarcely remember
Seeing such autumn colours
In all their splendour

And as the morning sun rises
Melting the mist
It puts a smile on my face
To see such a sight as this!

HOLD IT, HOLD IT!

As he tilted his head
I could see the holes
Filled with boogie
At the tip of his nose

And it would only take one sneeze
And I hope I'm not
Directly opposite
When he fires that snot!

JUST IN TIME!!

I caught the train this morning
By the skin of my teeth
Fussing round the house
I was late to leave

And now summer's nearly here
That early hot sun
Makes it difficult when one's late
And one has to run

I would not have been pleased
If the train had gone
It may have been a close call
But at least I got on!

OH JOYFUL SLOG!

Work is unavoidable, sometimes we love it,
other times ... well, you get the idea!

NOT LONG NOW

The week has suddenly become tolerable
Now that three days is already spent
But then next week I'll be saying
I just don't know where last week went

But with Thursday almost closing
And Friday on the way
All that's on my mind
Is to enjoy the next two days!

IS WORK WORTH THE TROUBLE?

It's nice to laze in bed
And watch the news
Catch up on the local and sports reviews
And I think, why get up?

I channel hop while adverts play
Watch bits of films, the soaps
And enjoy the start of the day
And still I think – Why get dressed?

I become engrossed with Channel 3
Some yummy dessert
Just right for me
And I'm reluctant to move

But as I check the clock it's not long 'til nine
And I realise I don't have very much time
To get to the bus stop and stand in line
And still I ask – Why did I get up?

But I had no real reason
To stay and shirk
The responsibilities allotted
To me at work

And yet the question
Remains on my tongue
Why did I not stay in bed
When the day had begun?

As I stand in the bus
With very little space
Close enough for someone
To yawn in my face

And then in the train
Squashed 'gainst the glass
There's not even enough space
For a fly to get pass

I think
Just for today
I could've avoided this farce
And stayed at home!

BLESSED FRIDAY!

The start of a weekend
Not a work day in sight
I can stay up late this evening
And well into the night

No getting up early
To iron my clothes
No setting three alarms
In case I over doze!

But I'll waste not one minute
There's a lot I've planned to do
And a list as long as my arm
That I'll attempt to get through

It doesn't take much
To get to my happy place
Just the thought of no commuting
Puts a smile on my face

I shall savour and enjoy
This two day break
This is one sweet tasting tonic
I'm ecstatic to take!

CELEBRATE THE WEEKEND!

It's Friday night
And I've waited all day
For the start of the weekend
Takeaway

Rush home from work
Get rid of the suit
The hustle and bustle
The smell of commute

Only one thing on my mind
Soon to be on my hips
Is whether to have pizza, Chinese
Or fish 'n' chips!

IT'S A LOVE THING....

Let your heart dream!

SWEET BUMPS

Ouch! My heart went bump
Th'moment I heard from you
Excitement welled up inside me
And grew and grew and grew

Like uncorking a bottle
Of sparkling champagne
The bubbles can't wait t'be released
It's sweet, it's insane

I just keep feeling
That sweet sweet pain
Ouch! There, my heart went bump
All over again!

CERTAINTIES

I was sure I couldn't like you
But inside I knew I did
I used every excuse under the sun not to
But I just couldn't get rid

Of the strong feelings growing
Every single day
That's making my heart miss you
That's blowing my mind away

I was so sure I couldn't like you
Though deep down I knew
With someone so gentle and considerate I
could
And was, falling hook, line and sinker for
you!

DRUNKEN BEAUTY

I'm inebriated by your beauty
Outside and in
And I'm sure that being loved by you
Would be sweeter than sin

The gentleness in your smile
Your caring nature's so extreme
The ecstasy I feel
Is only experienced in my dream

Your smile overwhelms me
Beyond any imaginable limit
And all I want to do
Is be bathed and be saturated in it!

SWEET NOTHINGNESS!

I could've sworn I felt you
Beside me in bed
I touched your body
I stroked your head

I heard that oh so familiar
Vibrating snore
That once used to annoy me
But not any more

I could've sworn I felt
Your hand touch mine
'Cause I felt that tingle
Down my spine

I could've sworn I felt
Your kiss goodnight
But when I opened my eyes
You were nowhere in sight!

WAITING FOR A MIRACLE!

I hugged my pillow
And depended upon
My dream to turn my pillow
Into a much longed for one

So, as I closed my eyes
I lay in the dark
And waited for
My dream to start

But as it began
I was only half way through
When I had to get up
And go to the loo!

SWEET MUSIC!

My heart just danced
Smiled and sang
The excitement hit
Going off with a bang

There was no warning
I'd feel like this
I'm shaking with pleasure
At euphoric bliss

But I wonder will the day
Ungraciously steal
This perfect dream
That seems so real!

ONE FINE DAY

I'm missing you and every day
The pain's a little bit more

I'm missing you and every day
It feels much worse than before

All the time I'm wishing
I hope and I pray

That if dreams come true
Then mine will too

And you'll be with me for real
One day!

MY INNER SMILE!

Smiling is making
Such a sweet banging on my heart
As you make me smile
So the pounding starts

And when the banging stops
The heart sustains
A painful but pleasurable
Sweet sweet pain!

WHERE ARE YOU?

I look to my left
And the bed is bare
I'm sure I felt you
Lying there

It felt pretty real
I'm certain I felt
A passion never experienced
That made my heart melt

But now I look
And I cry inside
'Cause nothing but a pillow
Lays beside!

YOU'RE EVERYWHERE

You're in every song I sing
Every note I play
Every word I read
Every moment of every day

Every programme I watch
Every morsel I eat
You still make me weak
From my head to my feet

You still hold me captive
You're in every breath of air
Every space I have you're in it
Every thought I have you're there

I want to say I love you
I want to say come home
I want to wrap my arms around you
And never leave you alone

I try to find a reason
Just one excuse to despise
But I know I'm only kidding myself
It's nothing but lies, all lies

For I know you are real
And very much a part
Whether I like it or not
You completely have my heart!

LIVING WITHOUT

How long will it take
For the hurt to subside
For the aching and sadness
To diminish inside

How many more nights
Must I have to go through
Lying awake
Trying to forget you?

HEALTHY WITHOUT YOU

I really do wish
We had never met
But now that we have
It's better I forget

And not relive
Those moments together
When I hoped those times
Would last forever

When happiness is so much
That it's painful to see
To forget about you
Is better for me!

GOSH! WHAT A NIGHT!

T'was a difficult night
I missed you more
Than any other night
I've been through before

I tried to distract
But it was hard to find
Anything adequate
To redirect my mind

So as I lay in the dark
With just the night in view
I welcomed my mind
And thoughts of you!

DREAMWORLD

I'm full of wishes
But alas it seems
That I must be content to forever
Live in my dreams

So, at morn
I close my eyes and see
Beautiful things
Surrounding me

And at night
When I lay down to rest
With you in my dreams
Is what I like best!

FIT FOR FOOD!

When all else fails, there's always cheese (and other comfort food).

MEANING OF LIFE

Eating is almost meaningless
If I don't have cheese
Brie, Blue Shropshire, Roquefort
Any one of these

I'll never grow tired
Of camembert, of cheddar
Just one of them daily
Makes me feel a whole lot better

For some it's ice cream
Or a chocolate bar
But for me a bit of cheese
Is the best by far!

HEALTHY v. HAPPINESS!

As I tuck into my cereal
And again try to convince
The recipient body
With a smile not a wince

Of the health issue benefits
I struggle to eat more
And think with each mouthful
That this thing taste like straw!

This daily ritual
Should make me happy
But I think alternative medication
Would make me less snappy

If one is to approach each new day
With sheer delight
Then why are my tastebuds
Putting up such a fight?

That healthy cereal
Made from wheat or oats
If not lodged 'tween y'teeth
Gets stuck in y'throat

Why can't healthy
Taste as nice
As a jam or ring doughnut
Not like al dente brown rice!

FIGHT THE URGE

I'm trying hard not
To eat to excess
When my body says no more spinach
Tummy knows best

When that yearning for chocolate
Is hard to hide
I fight to control
The build up inside

But though my heart is willing
My heart sadly lacks
The urge to resist
All those moreish snacks!

CHEESY

I love my cheese
But have you had moments when
You've eaten too fast and it gets stuck
In y' throat and then

Y'jaw goes into lock mode
And the cheese turns to glue
Slowly clogging up y'throat
Which makes swallowing hard to do

Then gagging begins
And y'eyes start to water
You're in panic mode
And y'breathing gets shorter

I would hate for it to be announced
On that fateful unavoidable day
That a sizeable lump of cheese
Took this girl's breath away!

IT'S ALL IN THE VEG!

How can I be unhealthy?
If they've taken the sugar out of my sweets
The salt off my crisps
The fat off my meat?

How can I not be healthy
When the crackling off my pork
Doesn't even come close
To my mouth or my fork?

When the crispy crunch
Of the chicken skin
Is not on the plate
That my dinner is in

When every bar of chocolate
The manufacturer's make
Is reduced by half
For my fat butt's sake?

How can I be unhealthy
If everything that's nice
They've lessened the sweet content
And upped the price?!

HOW CAN I BE UNHEALTHY?

PIPLESS

Where have all the seeds gone
In my pear
I'm sure a few years ago
Some were in there

The pips in my grapes
There's now not even one
There may not have been many
But they did at least have some

And as for water melon
That large green ball
Contained more seeds than people can hold
In the Royal Albert Hall

Now, if they could de-seed a pomegranate
Like all the rest
Then that fruit would definitely be
One of my best!

A ROCK, THE DEVIL AND ME

Now we're all well aware
That it has been said
'Tis better to eat wholemeal
Than white sliced bread

At times it's like eating
Straw every day
And I feel like I'm a horse
In the meadow eating hay

Why can't eating food
Be more fun
Not counting fat, sugar and calories
Down to the last crumb

I'm between a rock and a hard place
The devil, 'nd the deep blue sea
Whether I listen to my tastebuds
Or I listen to me!

IF MUSIC BE THE FOOD OF LIFE

EAT EAT EAT!

MY FAVOURITE DISH

The most beautiful, appetising
And arguably the best
Will beat any non-perishable
Will win every test

By far my most favourite
And I have a portion a day
To maintain my good mood
And keep the bad ones away

Will not go mouldy
Rancid or dry
It's delightful, palatable
And pleasing to the eye

I can have some anywhere
Whether I walk or drive
It's one of the few things I need
To keep me alive

Forget shopping, chocolates
And lemon meringue pie
Music is the only food
That gives me a high!

LOVE IS...

Love is so painful
Feel its urgency, its need
So desperate is its craving
That it soon turns to greed

Breathlessness, the stabbing
The terrible ache
And the heart pounding heavily
As if it will break

Panic attacks and the feeling
That life can't go on
Without the joy of dancing
Music and song!

NO COMPROMISE!

I could do without food
And I don't need to shop
And if ordered to not watch tv
I could easily stop

But take away my dancing
Music and song
Then all reason for living
Would definitely be gone!

GOOD SUBSTITUTION!

Let music block
All bad vibes
That bring us down
And interfere with our lives

Let those notes of inspiration
And beautiful sweet sounds
Flush away the negative
So only good surrounds

And, when all else fails
Let music reign
To encourage happiness
Where once was pain!

NO MUSIC – NO ME!

A bird with no wings
A harp without strings
A bell that never rings
I'm lost without music

A desert without sand
A leader but no band
A clock with one hand
I'm lost without music

A needle with no eye
A coconut but no shy
A rugby match with not one try
I'm lost without music!

TURNED ON BY YOU

After a hard day in the office
I come home to see
You quietly patiently
Waiting for me

I know you enjoy
When I turn you on
And, as soon as we touch
All tension is gone!

RICH AND CREAMY,
WET AND DREAMY!

Music is like feasting
On rich double cream
Or going to sleep
And waking up in a dream
Like sipping champagne
In a posh limousine
Or dangling your feet
In a cool running stream!

MY TIME TO THINK, CHILL AND UNWIND!

SIMPLY BEAUTIFUL!

How I love that blue sky
It makes me feel free
Let me ponder a while under
That lonesome tree.

I think God is good
To provide all this
And as I walk, my thoughts and me
I think this is bliss

A VIEW TO CHILL TO!

I look out my window
And onto the trees
And see the sky glistening
Among the leaves

It looks so pretty
Peeping through
And makes for a calming
Relaxing view

When the night is calm
And all is still
Those twinkling stars
Are such a thrill!

I LOVE HOME

It's always nice
To see the sights
The Severn Bridge
The New York lights

See different cultures
Have a change of cuisine
Visit places
You've never been

But no matter how exotic
A place you rest
It's true going back home
Is always best!

LET TIME STAND STILL

Stop the world
It's going too fast
The present comes quick
And even quicker the past

Please stop the world
And let me alight
To appreciate the beauty
Admire the sights

Let me disembark
I won't run away
I just want to enjoy it
For one extra day

Apply the brakes
Let me pause for a mo'
To consider the route
I'm destined to go

Let me separate myself
From those who scoff
Please stop the world
And let me get off!

ALL ROUND BEAUTY!

There's a distinct separation
'tween the sky and the clouds
And where the blue meets the trees
They are reverently bowed

And as I search in between
That mass of white
I behold the sun in all its glory
Shining bright!

DE-STRESSANT

When I go to the beach
I sit on the sand
Close my eyes
And dream of a land

Where bees don't sting
And dogs don't pooh
And, cause the owners don't clean up
It sticks to my shoe

But the place I'm in
Is where truth survives
Not jealousy, greed
And blatant lies

Where rhubarb crumble
Grows on trees
And a hundred and one different
Varieties of cheese

But I know right now
I cannot be here
It's gotten cooler, the tide's in
Almost reaching m'rear

But I'm more relaxed and refreshed
And because of my stay
I know I can get through
Another challenging day!

EASY LEARNING!

Standing at the bus stop
A white pigeon flew down
Searching for breakfast
With his beak to the ground

Then a grey one joined him
And together they fed
Upon left over burger
And stale bits of bread

I studied them eating
Happily away
And thought there's a lesson to be learned
In those pigeons today!

WHEN NOT IF!

When I can look out my window
And see a scene
That's refreshing, soothing
Not a mass of green
Over grown shrubbery
Expired brown leaves
A space that is continuously
Overtaken by weeds...

When I can look out of my window
And smile with a sigh
That what I'm viewing though expensive
Is pleasing to the eye
When I can look out of my window
In a calm relaxed state
Then I'll know the cost of this back yard
Was well worth the wait!

DANGEROUS CROSSING – THE FOX

Yesterday scampering
Bushy tailed
Darting across fields
And fences scaled

Yesterday scavenging
For food to eat
Frolicking in gardens
With flowers scented sweet

Moments before
A life so young
And now no more
To life is clung.

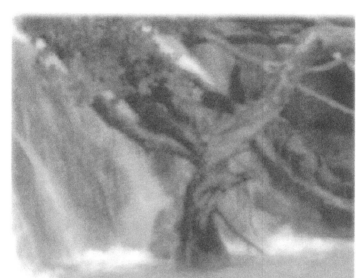

A DREAM COME TRUE?

As I closed my eyes
My mind ran free
And I lay there thinking
I was by the sea
Running then walking
Through warm soft sand
And, when I opened my eyes
There was a shell in my hand!

THE YEAR THAT WAS

No one can ignore the awful fate which hit the world in 2020 and we all found our own mechanism of coping; jogging, knitting, sewing, DIY, eating! Others on the other hand took to singing, whilst some of us wrote.....

THE PANDEMIC

YOU PANDEMIC YOU!
You force me to watch- every day news
I don't know what's a lie
Don't know what's true

YOU PANDEMIC YOU!
Why are you seeking to take lives this way
More and more people
Suffering each day

YOU PANDEMIC YOU!
What've we done to deserve this fate
You've taken away our privileges
At a disturbing rate

YOU PANDEMIC YOU!
Punish us no more - And let this cease
And return His people
To a land of peace...

YOU PANDEMIC YOU!

UNPREDICTED....

Who would've predicted
We'd spend most of last year
With such uncertainty
Sadness and fear

No hugs hello
No kisses goodbye
No one to explain
When we questioned why?

We've isolated, quarantined
We've been locked down
No visiting family
No shopping around town

But we will get through this
And when it is done
We can all resume our lives
And some long overdue fun!

UNWANTED QUIETNESS

Looking through my window
All is so still
No construction noise
No faint shrill

Of birds returning
To a country so fair
All is so still
No buzz in the air

Looking through my window
There's nothing so unappealing
As that silence so loud
An eerie eerie feeling

Not a silence of peace
Not relaxed or serene
But a sense of fear
Never before seen

The trouble we're in Lord
Only You can mend
And all over the world we're praying
That you'll have mercy and send

Blessings from above
And from on high descend
And heal all your people
Strangers, family and friends

129

From this which has surrounded
And confined us all
Please Oh Lord
Hear us as we call

Intervene we pray
Most earnestly
And cleanse our world from this dilemma
Lord please hear our plea.
Amen

GET IT ANYWHERE!

I'll shop anywhere
Without a queue
I'll purchase anything as long as
I'm not waiting behind you

Don't care the brand
Whatever the price that's fine
I'll buy s'long as I don't
Have to stand in line

I'll buy veg from the chemist
And cereal from there too
Even cheese from the car showroom
As long as I don't have to queue!

MUST HAVE

The only thing that bothered me
Is would I have enough mayonnaise
At home to keep me going
While in the lockdown phase

It accompanies my potatoes
It smothers my chips
But I wish when travelling through
It didn't make a detour to my hips!

But I'm getting in a panic
If when I go join the shopping queue
And finally get in to empty shelves
What am I gonna do?

But perhaps it's no a bad thing
With no mayonnaise to buy
These pounds will finally fall
From stomach and from thighs!

STINKING LOCKDOWN!

I hope all in lockdown
Took that time
To eat nothing but onions, garlic
And drink loadsa wine

'Cause when restrictions are lifted
And we're released from our quarters
It'll be back to salad sarnies
And a glass of water!

GOT IT CO-VERED!

Antibacterial in my throat
Disinfectant up my nose
Gel on my hands
So you'd naturally suppose

That I'm protected fully
From anything that may loom
Outside in the open
Or here in my room

So I shouldn't be threatened
Where there's visible skin
'Cause the virus has been prevented
From ever getting in

It matters not if I suffocate
Who's gonna care
'cause the mask and shield I have on
Won't let in sufficient air

As long as I'm suitably covered
From the current clime
I'm happy to be starved of oxygen
At this present time!

THE QUIET WAR!

It's not country against country
But the world is at one
Fighting to survive
Not with bombs or guns ...

A silent battle
That has made us unite
In suffering, in mourning
But we will win this fight

As The Holy One suffered
The cross and the pain
To rise above all others
And forever reign

So will we
Rise from the ground
And conquer that which is trying
To bring us down

Our prayers will be answered
Just wait and see
Pretty soon this world will overcome
To victory!

BELIEVING IN.....

We all believe in something, be it the universe, our leaders, religion, our family, we will always question, but will still look to those in whom we trust for support and guidance to help us through.....

A MILLION REASONS TO SMILE –
Here are just a few of 'em!

Smile 'cause God heard last night
When you knelt to pray
Smile 'cause as a result
You woke up today

Smile 'cause you can hear
And talk, and see
Smile, 'cause you've friends
And family

Smile, when things are hard
And life gets tough
Smile 'cause He'll bring you through
When the going's rough

Smile 'cause when wars
Tear countries apart
You can smile 'cause you know you have
Peace in your heart

So, when you want to frown
Just take awhile
And find one of those million reasons
To sit up and smile!

SOMETIMES

Sometimes I think
How should I pray
How should I sit
What should I say

Sometimes I wonder
Does He listen, does He see
Will He continually
Watch over me?

SHEER MADNESS

I don't think I'm mad
I know I am
I'm mad about cheese
And oven roasted lamb

Cakes and pastries
Yorkshire pud
Baked potatoes mashed with butter
Are finger licking good

But the three to excite
And stir the most
Are the Father, Son
And Holy Ghost!

I WONDER HOW?

How can a tree grow
Hundreds of feet tall
From a seed or sapling
So very small?

Their trunk so strong
So lush and green
From no other sustenance,
'cept when the rains have been

Who else could create
Who else could devise
A wonder so beautiful
To a person's eyes
But God!

WHY, WHY, WHY?

Why is it we can't live
On this earth so vast
We fight about land
We argue over class

Why can't we live harmoniously
Together in this place
And not quarrel over money
Or disagree over race

We're selfish in our attitudes
Is that how we were taught?
Uncaring about others
In our deeds and our thoughts

Lord make us mindful
In what we do and say
Considerate to one another
Each and every day.

AND, SO, LIFE GOES ON!

As Percy Byxshe Shelley once said:

If Winter comes, can Spring be far behind?

SUN – NO BUGS – FUN

Winter and rain
Snow and ice
If you don't visit for four months
That would be nice

Sun, not too hot
Come every day
But dear bees and bugs
Please stay away!

WHETHER WEATHER

The weatherman says
It'll be 16 degrees
But I don't think the sky says the same

Its big cotton-like clouds
Seem menacing to me
And look set to burst out with more rain

But I've no choice I suppose
And shall have to rely
On the forecast and hope it holds true

'Cause I've forgotten my brolly
And I'll not be amused
If I get wet going home through and through!

A FLOWER BY ANY OTHER NAME IS A WEED!

The weeds run rampant in the garden
Why does it have to rain
As fast as I pull them out
They grow back again

When house plants are nurtured, fed
And looked after with care
Not one of them look as healthy
As those weeds blooming out there

I'm hard pressed to dig under the shingle
Membrane, sand and slate
But these little hardy plants pop up with ease
At an alarming rate

Perhaps I'll pot the weeds
And bring them all inside
Give them a fancy name
And watch 'em grow indoors with pride!

RAINBOW RAINBOW

Rainbow, oh rainbow
How do you stay
So high in the sky
On such a wet day

How come you don't fall
And break into two
And make one rainbow with red
The other with blue?

I love all your colours, red yellow
Blue and green
Though most of the others
Cannot easily be seen

A spectacular sight
Making people go aaaaaah
As in awe they watch you
So high so far

When it rains I know
If I search the sky
You will always be found
And I'll smile with a sigh!

A LOST CAUSE!

I toss and turn
Many times in bed
Continually fluff the pillows
That soothe my head

Do I do this
Whilst counting sheep
Or is this done
Whilst I'm asleep?

As I hum the tune playing
On the radio
I'm tapping to the beat
With all ten toes

I'm weary, I'm spent
And need to rest my brain
So I can wake refreshed and repeat
The work sequence over again

I roll to the left
Then to the right
But there's not a hint of sleep
Anywhere in sight

Even the sheep
Have left me to cope
I can't hear a bleat
They've given up hope

Though my eyes are closed
My mind's still alert
Perhaps it can rest
While it's still at work

It's becoming critical
The sun's beginning to peep
At this rate I'll be waking up
While still trying to sleep!

WHAT COST TO SMILE?

If we smile a little bit
It may just catch on
And if we laugh a whole lot
Others may just tag along

The world may seem a little brighter
If only for a while
So, wherever you are today
Just give a little smile!

DO I OR NOT, THAT IS THE QUESTION?

I'd still like to know
If I actually sleep
But I can't stay awake long enough
To get a peep

Another question on my mind
Is do I snore
But whilst my eyes are closed
I'm just not sure!

As I shut my eyes
My ears are closed too
So I can't hear a thing
Of what I may actually do

Ignorance is bliss
As the saying goes
So I'll continue in oblivion
To whatever happens while I dose!

SLOW DOWN!

Slow down take time
To enjoy your day
Don't let the pace of life
Take your fun away!

ALL TOGETHER

We're all in this together
We only have one earth
All in this together
Have been since birth

Let's try to live together
Be kind to everyone
Remember we're all somebody's daughter
Mother, father or son

Let's try to live together
There's room here for us all
Let's not waste time in idle pettiness
Or enjoy watching another man fall

There's really no other planet
With electricity water and gas
Dustmen and supermarkets
Taxis and buses en mass

Please try and live together
In peace and harmony
Because until I get to Heaven
There's no other place I'd rather be!

And That's Your Lot (for now)!

Acknowledgement

Many thanks to Barbara Donaldson for her support in providing opportunities for audiences to hear my verses (of which none, I am relieved to say, ever felt compelled to make a hasty exit in midstream!), and to her husband, the Late Rev'd Jim Donaldson, for "going on at me" to publish some of my verses – keep shufflin' up there Jim!

And not forgetting, my publishers, Selfishgenie, for taking a chance on me and without whom this volume of verse you wouldn't be reading.

About AngieD

Born and bred in North London and Enfield, experiencing life in Essex before finally settling, for the time being, a little further north than Watford.

Who knew her first poem about a mynah bird would evolve, years later, into a whole host of verses?

Whether commuting into London or staying local, a writing book is never far away.

Whether it's her passion for music, love of cheese or appreciation that most things in life are beautiful or will bring a smile, it may be 2.00am or 2.00pm but if it is perceived, it will be documented!

And Now

Both the author AngieD and Selfishgenie Publishing hope that you have enjoyed reading this book and that you have found it useful.

You can e-mail AngieD at **angied@selfishgenie.com**

Please tell people about this eBook, write a review or mention it on your favourite social networking sites.

For further titles that may be of interest to you please visit the Selfishgenie Publishing website at **selfishgenie.com** where you can join our mailing list so that we can keep you up to date with all our latest releases (or maybe that should be 'escapes').

Printed in Great Britain
by Amazon

13475484R00092